Ripple Zone

James Hartsock

ISBN 978-1-64492-328-3 (paperback)
ISBN 978-1-64492-329-0 (digital)

Christian Faith Publishing, Inc.
832 Park Avenue
Meadville, PA 16335
www.christianfaithpublishing.com

Printed in the United States of America

Through the Blood

Through the blood we are made complete,
It's the only way to escape eternal defeat.
Jesus was a real man among men,
He knew He was the only one to free us from sin.
Imagine the fear He must have felt,
At the hand He had been dealt.
Even though He never would complain,
It must have truly been a terrible strain.
To know He was totally pure,
And yet He was the only cure.
What courage and strength it must have took,
On that cross through the ages He could look.
At all the deeds we've done through the years,
He knew the price was greater than His fears.
Never calling the angels to come down in a flood,
Knowing the only answer was through the Blood.

Born to Bleed

What is this world coming to?
Good honest people are always too few.
Addicts out looking for the next quick fix,
Teenage girls on street corners turning tricks.
Sisters against sisters—brothers against brothers,
Newborn babies killed by their own mothers.
Everyone seems to be out for number one,
Never thinking of turning to God's Son.
In God's own image we were made,
How could we forget the price He paid?
The world is in such a dreadful state,
Filled with so much sex, violence, and hate.
The Only way out has already been sent,
But we must humble ourselves and repent.
Jesus Christ will fill our every need,
Because He was born for us simply to bleed.

Totally Amazed

The Lord has started in my heart a fire,
To serve Him has become my only desire.
My life as His new creation has truly started,
From my old and sinful nature, I have departed.
Even now I am still totally amazed,
That when through the years He gazed.
He was looking directly at me,
Sometimes I think, "How can this be?"
That for me He was beaten, mocked, and torn,
Yet He loved me even before I was born.
Now I must give Him everything I am,
Because for me He gave His Precious Lamb.

Truly Believe

Beware my friend time is winding down,
It is time to quit acting like a clown.
What if tomorrow would never come,
Have you stopped to think of the ransom?
That Jesus Christ paid for your sin,
Death, but satan could not win.
Three days later He rose from the dead,
But only thoughts of the flesh crowd your head.
Why do we continue to sin again and again,
Allowing ourselves to be one of satan's kin?
We must arise above all the petty issues,
Listen to the Lord and start paying our dues.
If we want Jesus to act as our attorney,
Only He can plea for our eternal journey.
To the Father He takes our pleas,
And from our sin He gladly frees.
Those who ask and truly believe,
Eternal salvation is what we receive.

Use Me

I want with all of my heart to be one of God's chosen,
Not to just sit in a pew as if I am frozen.
Lord draw me close show me what to do,
Your will for me— please give me a clue.
Help me be patient—wait on Your timing,
My excitement rises always climbing.
Lord use me in Your eternal divine plan,
If I could help save the soul of just one man.
Oh, to hear my Lord say, "This one loves me,"
Even when I fall and fail Him miserably.
Pick me up Lord from off the ground,
Get me ready to fight the next round.

Your Love

Is it possible for us to understand
the full extent of Your love?
Watching all the evil we do as You sit in Heaven far above.
Could we blame You if You turned Your back on us forever?
But Your love is an unbreakable chain sin could never sever.
The Bible tells us of the lifestyle we should be living,
Instead of thinking of ourselves all the
time we should be giving.
Your precious Son gave us everything He possibly could,
If we simply had called Him, by our
side He would have stood.
And yet we continue to stumble through live hopelessly lost,
Blindly thinking we must better
ourselves no matter the cost.
If we could just stop for a minute and simply ask You,
We would see what the awesome power of Your love can do.

More Like Jesus

Forever upon the Rock I will lean,
The power of His love I have seen.
Delivering me from the hell I lived in,
He forgave and took away all my sin.
All I have is my life to give,
Help me always for you to live.
Everything I am or ever will be,
I owe to the One who hung on the tree.
Jesus use me to fulfill Your plan,
Thru the power of Your Spirit I'll do all I can.

Always There

Always there lending a hand,
Always there in sinking sand.
Always there to teach and to guide,
Always there right by my side.
Always there in joy and in tears,
Always there to calm all my fears.
Always there when I think I'm alone,
Always there calling me Your own.
Always there as You said You'd be,
Always there Your promise to me!

Proof of You

When I look around can there be any doubt,
That only You could plan the world out.
From the beautiful glow of a shiny full moon,
To the graceful drifting of a tropical sand dune.
The bright colors we see in the crisp fall,
Prove to me You had Your hand in it all.
Song birds singing on a warm summer day,
Little children laughing happily as they play.
Gently rolling waves washing up on the shore,
Majestic mountain peaks where eagles soar.
All creation lives and breathes because of You,
The result of Your unconditional love so true.

Not Worthy

Not worthy to lace the string on His sandal,
And yet He still gives the light of His eternal candle.
Not worthy to walk by His sword-pierced side,
And yet He is with me in every task I've tried.
Not worthy to hold His nail-pierced hand,
And yet by my side He will always stand.
Not worthy to call upon His precious name,
And yet for my sins He took the blame.
Not worthy to receive His divine love,
And yet He gives it constantly from Heaven above.
Not worthy to feel His Holy Spirit's power,
And yet at my feet He makes demons cower.
Not worthy to kneel at His Holy feet,
And yet He died to make my life complete.
Not worthy to call Jesus my friend,
And yet He is with me even to the end.

Closer to You

Closer to You is where I truly want to be,
Wrapped in the comfort of Your arms for eternity.
I was lost in the world for so many years,
Blinded by a sea of unnecessary tears.
Thank You for the day You opened my eyes,
Now I am no longer subject to satan's lies.
From his cruel hands I have been set free,
Because You gave Your only Son to sanctify me.
You alone are truly worthy of all my praise,
Please help me to follow in all of Your ways.
I need You my God in everything I do,
That is why I strive daily to be closer to You.

One Day

One day when I get to the other side,
I'll see the One who sent the cleansing tide.
That set my sinful broken heart free,
The One who died on the cross for me.
Oh, such joy when I finally see His face,
Standing in the presence of His saving grace.
Words can't express what I'll feel that day,
When He calls me to my home in Heaven to stay.
Forever with the Lamb and His Father the King,
Their praises night and day I'll eternally sing.

Alone

Frightened and alone standing in the cold,
I wonder if she has ever been told?
Someone loves her just as she is,
Longing for her to become one of His.
Love that is pure of the deepest kind,
Trapped on the street will she ever find.
Peace to fill the empty space inside,
Or an end to all the tears she's cried?
Send a laborer even though they are few,
Lord have mercy—call her to You.

Walk the Walk

To serve the Lord you can't just talk the talk,
You have to look to Him and always walk the walk.
Praising Him on Sunday then forgetting Him on Monday?
No my friend it just doesn't work that way.
It can't be just a one-day-a-week thing,
Surrender to Him daily truly make Him King.
If it's up to Heaven you want to be raised,
The Father and Son must always be praised.
Let the Holy Spirit guide you in everything you do,
So the Lord may know that your love for Him is true.
Don't be weak and crumble like a piece of chalk,
Draw your strength from Jesus and always walk the walk.

Eternal Loser

All satan knows how to do is cheat and lie,
That is why on God's word we must rely.
To help you get thru times of temptation,
Show the loser you are a new creation.
Never will he enjoy any heavenly treasure,
So the only way he can get any pleasure.
Is to try and steal the joy we have found,
Trembling when he hears the joyous sound.
Of the saints heralding Jesus's return,
He'll be back in hell forever to burn.
The best he can do is be a pathetic user,
Because he already knows he's the eternal loser.

Here I Am

Here I am Lord use me for Your glory,
Don't let me be part of the same old story.
Thinking Sunday is all I'll ever need,
That is not why Your Son was willing to bleed.
Let me praise and worship Him every day,
It's the only way I can even try to repay.
The price He paid for my eternal salvation,
And the person I am as His new creation.
Father, I give You my life to use,
For it is no longer mine to abuse.
Take it and use it to do only Your will,
Save me from the one who will lie, cheat, and kill.
Worthy of all my praise is Your Precious Lamb,
So I say to You, Father, "Here I Am!"

I Praise You

There is no other reason for me to take a breath,
Than to praise You always even until my death.
I can't possibly give You all the praise You deserve,
But my love for You will never falter or swerve.
I pray You will take what I can lovingly give,
Everything I am even the life that I live.
Use it Father for the fulfillment of Your will,
Fill my mouth with the words let my feet not be still.
Until the good news of Your Son has been heard,
And we receive the salvation promised in Your word.
Father I lift Your name upon high,
Singing Your praises until the day I die.

Passing Pleasures

Thou are worthy most Holy One,
Eternal life comes only from Your Son.
Your precious gift to all of mankind,
A truer love we could never find.
When will we open our eyes,
And stop believing all of satan's lies?
All we need is right in front of our face,
Given freely to us thru His mercy and grace.
Why do we have to make it so hard?
Jesus already played the final card.
When He rose from the fiery pit called hell,
And yet our souls we continue to sell.
For the passing pleasures of this earth,
Remember in Heaven they have no worth.
Send them back to the father of lies,
In exchange for a home where no one dies.

Treasures or Pleasures

How long will we be willing to sacrifice
our heavenly treasures,
For the temporary joy of these sinful earthly pleasures.
The Lord is calling out from Heaven to us every day,
But we let the things of this world distract us get in the way.
It is so hard for us to make the right choice,
If we never take the time to listen to His voice.
We need to come before Him—fall on our face,
Then everything else will have to take it's place.
If we keep saying, "I'll get around to it tomorrow,"
We may find ourselves forever drowning in sorrow.
No one is perfect but surely we can see,
Our Lord wants us to be with Him for eternity.

Let the Lions Roar

It is written in God's Holy Word,
That through Jesus Christ we are cured.
We should be bold as a lion,
So let's stop our whinin' and cryin'.
Let the Lions Roar!
Praise God from whom all blessings flow,
And thank Him for the day we came to know.
Jesus Christ as our Lord and master,
Now we are saved from eternal disaster.
Let the Lions Roar!
The disaster of a place called hell,
Where satan landed when he fell.
From Heaven and all of God's grace,
No longer able to look at His face.
Let the Lions Roar!
The time beloved is truly at hand,
For the body of Christ to take a stand.
The wages of sin we can no longer afford,
Cry out to the world, "Jesus is Lord!"
Let the Lions Roar!

Anointed and Appointed

Through God's grace and love we are anointed,
To help save His children we are appointed.
Confess the Lord Jesus with your mouth,
In the north, east, west, and south.
Sent forth to do God's will,
I pray we will never be still.
While there are souls out there to save,
We cannot let them go to the grave.
Never hearing of the joys Jesus can bring,
That He is the one and only true King.
We must rally God's army and be heard,
Reach out to others—tell them His word.
Put your hands to the plow and have no fear,
When you speak His name He's always near.

Experience the Difference

If you're tired of the lifestyle that you live,
Come experience the difference Jesus can give.
He can make the same old life become brand new,
When you make Him the center of everything you do.
After you feel His love deep in your heart,
You'll know it's time for you to play your part.
In trying to make the world a better place for all,
And to teach your children to answer God's call.
It's up to us to show them the only Way,
To be freed from the temptations of today.
If He can change someone like me,
He can make changing you seem easy.
Come experience the difference Jesus can make,
The chains that bind you only He can break.

Salvation or Damnation

Jesus walked this earth for only one reason,
So that we could have peace in every season.
Thru His ministry, death, and resurrection,
We are shown that there is only one direction.
That God wants all of mankind to go,
I truly wish we all could know.
The power of His precious blood and name,
Maybe then we'd have a clue about this game.
Our daily struggle we call life,
Where a child kills another with a knife.
Why can't we all just get along,
And try to do each other no wrong?
Jesus Christ made the ultimate sacrifice,
Why can't we understand He paid the price?
For our joy and eternal salvation,
Don't give it up for eternal damnation.

Slow Down

Does life always have you in a rush?
Maybe it is time for you to just hush.
Stop and let the Lord be Lord again,
Without His help you can't ever win.
Busy schedule got you running to-and-fro,
Wondering why your walk doesn't grow.
Slow down take some time to pray,
Open His Word—what's He have to say?
Regain the peace that made you whole,
Talk to the One who saved your soul.

Have No Fear

Go forth and have no fear,
For the Lord holds you dear.
He will bless you in everything you do,
Because He knows your love is true.
Wherever your journey may lead,
Take with you this simple creed.
Give the Lord your love all your days,
Give His worthy Lamb all your praise.
Look to Him and you will never thirst,
Because it was He who loved you first.

Let God Lead

Doing God's will can be like riding a bike,
Sometimes we don't always get to do what we like.
Your bike has to be a bicycle made for two,
If you want the Lord to bless you in everything you do.
The Lord must be the one in the driver's seat,
It's the only way He can make your life complete.
Put your feet to the pedals—do the work,
For you never know where the enemy may lurk.
Submit to the Lord—let Him steer,
Look always to Him and have no fear.
If you do these things He'll be by your side,
A promise He made when His precious Son died.
He must be the center if you are going to succeed,
The only way to make it is to let God lead.

I Believe

I believe Jesus is the One and Only Way,
I believe He is the potter I am the clay.
I believe I am saved by His eternal grace,
I believe someday I will see His holy face.
I believe He fulfilled His Father's glorious plan,
I believe He wants to save the soul of every man.
I believe He died and rose from the dead,
I believe every single word He ever said.
I believe He is at the Father's right hand,
I believe on my behalf He always takes a stand.
I believe He is the only reason I wake,
I believe He is every breath that I take.

You in Me

Lord, when others look at me,
Let it be You that they see.
Your love shining through this outer man,
Help me reveal the joy of Your plan.
It's nothing I can do on my own,
The strength comes from You alone.
Put words in my mouth as I speak,
Make a warrior out of what was weak.
May my life be a sacrifice to You,
Helping others find the One love so true.

It's Up to You

The price has already been paid,
Now a decision must be made.
Will you continue your sinful ways,
Or choose to give Jesus all your praise?
"Forgive them Father" is what He said,
While He hung on the cross and bled.
Three days later He rose from the grave,
The road to Heaven only He could pave.
Do you want a love that is always true?
He has left the choice totally up to you.

I Surrender All

Sometimes I don't know why it seems,
The Lord has answered all of my dreams.
I know it's not because of anything I've done,
It has to be the blood of His precious Son.
I can't ever explain why He loves me so much,
But I know I can't live without His cleansing touch.
Ever since the day I chose to follow Him,
I know I am never alone when things get dim.
He can do for you what He's done for me,
He's the same today, tomorrow, and for eternity.
As His new creation my life's complete,
I surrender all—kneeling at His feet.

Between the Lines

If you read between the lines,
Someone has paid all your fines.
For the sinful life you led,
He went to the cross and bled.
Knowing there was no other way,
Through love He refused to disobey.
He could have called the angels anytime,
But He chose to die guilty of no crime.
Scars on His back are the lines I speak of,
Read between them to find the purest love.
Look past the many tears you have cried,
Only Jesus can fill the empty space inside.

For Me

You knew me before I was even born,
For me Your body was ripped and torn.
Not thinking of Yourself but only of me,
You went to a place they call Calvary.
A cry to Your Father could have stopped all Your pain,
But You offered Your blood to cleanse sin's ugly stain.
Now through that blood I'm a changed man,
Sharing the Good News whenever I can.
On the strength of Your Spirit I've come to depend,
My Lord, My Savior, My Very Best Friend.

The Dash

As we constantly dash from here to there,
Concentrating on things we think need our care.
Losing sight of what we should really do,
Acts of kindness and love are far too few.
Look in a cemetery one thing's the same,
On the stone or marker it's not the name.
Slow down, open your eyes, and look around,
A secret for life is waiting to be found.
It's not the date but what's in-between,
A small little dash what does it mean?
Each day you're given is a gift from God,
What did you do on the path you trod?
Was your dash a blur or a never-ending race?
Did you see the one who needed a warm embrace?
Your dash is the story of what you've done,
The winner is not the fastest runner who's run.
Did your dash make the world a better place?
Can others see in you the light of God's grace?

Beware of Satan

The master of this world is a liar,
Trying to capture you in his eternal fire.
He will promise you worldly pleasures,
But seeks to steal your Heavenly treasures.
Anger, greed, and lust are his tools,
Used to make us his sinful fools.
Trying desperately to keep us from our Savior,
Doing everything to corrupt our behavior.
With deceit and treachery he blinds,
Always trying to cloud our minds.
His gifts can give you a thrill,
But it is your soul he wishes to kill.
He is no match for Jesus and the Holy Ghost,
Only if we love the Lamb's Father the most.
Beware of satan and his lies my friend,
Without Jesus he will have you in the end.

Give Jesus a Try

Until the day I asked Jesus in,
And He took away my grief and sin.
I was only being an arrogant fool,
Drowning in the world's cesspool.
Thinking I could make it on my own,
Walking around with a heart of stone.
The thought never crossing my mind,
That I could be one of God's kind.
But Jesus reached down and with one single blow,
His glory, honor, and power to me He did show.
He crushed the stone wall around my heart,
And said, "From this day forward you'll have a new start."
He did it for me—He can do it for you,
So if life's got you down and blue.
Pick up your head and look to the sky,
Just give my best friend Jesus a try.

Different Ways

You can serve the Lord in many different ways,
Some will preach His word the rest of their days.
Others can praise Him with their song,
Lifting their voices to Heaven all day long.
Your gift may be the ability to comfort others,
Still others could be good Godly mothers.
Teaching your children good from bad,
Could be a gift of a God-fearing dad.
Some help those in need only because they care,
Expecting nothing but receiving a whispered prayer.
Others simply let His light shine thru them,
Giving smiles and hugs when things get dim.
In God's eyes all these deeds are the same,
Only if they are done to glorify Jesus's name.

Deny Yourself

Everyone feels the weight of the world sometimes,
Just believe Jesus paid for our crimes.
And your soul can be set free,
Because for us He hung on that tree.
He died to cover us in His precious blood,
That we may be protected in any kind of flood.
All we have to do is make a simple choice,
To deny yourself and lift up our voice.
The burden of our own cross we must bear,
To go out with others and the gospel share.
It is what Jesus told us to do,
If we want Him to say "Friend, I know you."
When someday before His Father we come,
And expect to enter into His holy kingdom.

About to Drown

As we strive to get to the next level,
Around every corner is a different devil.
Trying to break and drag us down,
Making us feel like we are about to drown.
Problems of the world piled upon our backs,
Stumbling from their constant evil attacks.
Laughing at us like we are some kind of joke,
While never thinking of taking Jesus's yoke.
Once we do that the burden can be lifted,
As we become one of the few who are gifted.
To have Jesus forever by our side,
Delivering us from life's every tide.
Praying our actions reflect the words we say,
Let us praise the worthy Lamb every day.

Change Me

I lay my life down on your altar,
Praying always that I will not falter.
As I struggle with my worst enemy,
The part of me that must die daily.
If only "I" could stay out of the way,
A bigger part in Your plan I could play.
There are so many souls out there to save,
Not yet knowing what Jesus Christ gave.
They wonder through life alone and lost,
Help me reach them no matter the cost.
Change me into what You need me to be,
So I can tell them the story of Calvary.
How Jesus Christ lived and died for them,
To save them from a life that's become so dim.

Eternally Cool

Ordinary people have the most extraordinary gift,
It is the ability they have to give you a lift.
When they tell you how they feel,
That their love for you is truly real.
Like when your children smile at you,
Believing in everything you may do.
Or the feeling you get from that special someone,
As you realize your searching is finally done.
God can make you feel even better than that,
Because Jesus is the center of where it is at.
He laid down His life for all of mankind,
A truer love than His you will never find.
Open up your eyes and be set free,
If you want to be cool for eternity.

No Matter the Cost

We must help the Lord win the lost,
No matter what to us the cost.
Right or wrong which path will they choose?
They're shooting each other for a pair of shoes.
Satan got them to take prayer out of schools,
Now he's laughing as he steals our kid's souls.
It's time to get up and take a stand,
For the return of the Lord is close at hand.
This movement must go from the pulpit to the pew,
Because it is going to take more than just a few.
The army of God must truly unite,
If we expect to win this crucial fight.
I know it will be worth all the scars,
To take back what is rightfully ours.
As parents and children once again become one,
Jesus will be able to say "Friends, well done."

Pick Up Your Cross

When are we ever going to learn,
Our gifts in Heaven we must earn?
Wanting only the things that please us,
Never taking time for Jesus.
Only crying out when we need Him,
Asking for light when things get dim.
We must show Him we really care,
By saying more than just an occasional prayer.
Daily we must seek and give Him praise,
So let's stop walking around in a daze.
Blinded by all of satan's lies,
It's time to let go of worldly ties.
Turn to Him and pick up your cross,
Let satan suffer yet another loss.

My Friend

I have finally found a true Friend,
His love for me is never pretend.
He took a beating that was meant for me,
Then they crucified Him on a tree.
He died to give me eternal life,
Even when my path is filled with strife.
I know I can always turn to Him,
Because He simply said, "Father, forgive them."
All I had to do was truly believe,
Now my side He will never leave.
And despite all my sinful behavior,
He's always there My Friend, My Savior.

One's Love

In a world that is so hard and cold,
The story of One's love must be told.
One who loved me even before we ever met,
By whose hands the foundations of the earth were set.
His never-ending love, mercy, and grace,
Have placed a smile on a battle-scarred face.
Now instead of fighting my sisters and brothers,
This warrior has vowed to try and help others.
Find the love that forever changed this heart,
Only through One can you have a new start.
Turn to Him and for you He'll do the same,
Just call on my friend—Jesus is His name.

Christ in You

Can people really see Christ in you?
Does it reflect in everything you do?
In some it is easy to see,
Never saying "What about me?"
Always putting the needs of others first,
Giving water to those who thirst.
Do people say when they look at me,
"I'd like some of that Christianity?"
If we are truly living our life right,
They will surely see His light.
Oh, what joy and happiness we can bring,
When we lead someone new to the King.
Does the love of Jesus shine through,
So that people know Christ is in you?

Run to Him

Run to Him don't just walk,
He will give you peace not idle talk.
He will lift you up and take your pain,
When He sees your back starting to strain.
Under the heavy load you try to bear,
Just look around He's everywhere.
Run to Him and be set free,
He is the only Way to find Victory.
The price for your life has already been paid,
Run to Him and a new creature will be made.
From the old will come the new,
Listen to this saved sinner—take this cue.
If life's battles have gotten you down,
Run to Him and receive a crown.

Our Lives Are Paid For

We owe Jesus Christ everything,
He is the one and only true King.
How can we ignore what He did for us?
He did not whine or cause a fuss.
Jesus quietly did what He must,
So we could be forgiven of our lust.
Meekly He carried out His Father's task,
"Why me?" He would never ask.
He loved us before we were born,
Only to be beaten, broken, and torn.
Our lives to Him we must give,
If in Heaven we expect to live.
Because on a cross made from a tree,
He died to pay for you and me.

Lift Me Up

Show me the error of my ways,
So I can serve You all of my days.
There are so many souls left to save,
Not yet knowing what Jesus gave.
They walk through life lost and alone,
Bitter hearts growing harder than stone.
If I'm going to try to stand in the gap,
Must avoid being caught in life's petty crap.
Everywhere I turn so much resistance,
With Your Spirit's power I'll go the distance.
Lift me up help me to walk straight,
So I may lead others to Heaven's gate.

God's Love

In all of the universe it is the most powerful force,
He will use it to chart our individual course.
The Father knows your every want, need, and desire,
Come and let Him fill you with the Holy Ghost's fire.
Even though we are not worthy to hold His hand,
For us He will always take a stand.
Against satan's army of darkness and death,
The battle was won when He restored Jesus's breath.
Jesus hung on the cross dying and groaning,
So we could be saved by the power of His blood's atoning.
The love of the Father for His Son,
Can belong to each and every one.
Never any favoritism He loves us all the same,
All we have to do is call upon His name.
The sacrifice He made we can never repay.
And yet God's love is with us every second of the day.

It Is Time

It is time to get out of our pew,
The will of the Father we must do.
Jesus came to earth for only one reason,
Not spreading the Gospel is an act of treason.
On the day He came into your heart,
You made a commitment to play your part.
Now we must put our fears aside,
And with His Holy Spirit abide.
So many out there broken and lost,
We must show them Jesus at any cost.

Winning Side

The war is over, but the battle still rages,
Sin can drag us down locking us in cages.
We must carry on the work Jesus started,
He gave His church the power before He departed.
As we look at the world thru Jesus's eyes,
Only then can we see thru satan's lies.
Jesus already defeated death, hell, and the grave,
By refusing to fail us, mankind He did save.
When temptation comes causing spirit and flesh to collide,
Don't ever give up friend - we're on the winning side.

Daily Gifts

Oh Lord the beautiful moonlit sky who could paint,
Wisely set high above so no human hand can taint.
The precious daily gifts You've freely given to us,
If we will only open our eyes and look past all the fuss.
Simple things like a single flower or a star-filled sky,
Show us that nothing escapes Your watchful eye.
Colorful sunsets may bring an end to each day,
But these are only signs of the message You relay.
Your unfailing love for us can be seen all around,
By opening our heart to You completeness is found.

Better Place

Is the world a better place because you were here?
Do the ones you love know that you hold them dear?
Life flies by and time slips away,
Do the best you can with each passing day.
Humble yourself and put others first,
So many needs they hunger and thirst.
Most not even understanding what they need,
Did you take the time to plant that seed?
A warm smile, a friendly hug, or a simple phone call,
To us it may only seem like something so small.
Share some love and hope—there's nothing to fear,
Is the world a better place because you were here?

Lord Help Me

Jesus you must increase in everything I do,
Lord help me when I struggle to keep my eyes on You.
When things fall apart and everything goes wrong,
Lord help me to remember when I'm weak You are strong.
Life's storms crash against me sometimes so hard to stand,
Lord help me to never forget the "Footprints in the Sand."
You pick me up, dust me off, and set me on my feet,
Lord help me to tell others You made my life complete.
So as I press forward please ignore my sinful state,
Lord help me sing Your praises when I enter Heaven's gate.

The River

The river that flows from the Father's throne,
Can melt even the hardest heart made of stone.
No matter where you've been or what you've done,
Forgiveness has already been bought by His Only Son.
He loves you so much He was willing to die,
That's why He did nothing when they cried, "Crucify!"
The Lord Jesus Christ is the Only Way to be free,
This river of His Spirit is a gift to you and to me.
It's totally free just accept and ask Him in,
Oh, what a feeling—to be delivered from sin!

The Gift

In Bethlehem He was born,
Soon to become an object of scorn.
Hated by those He had come to save,
Crucified then placed in a grave.
It was time for the world to know,
God was about to steal the show.
He breathed life back into His Son,
To show He was the Only One.
Who can give the gift of salvation,
To you, me, and every generation.

The Battle Is Won

Lord I wonder, "Are You calling me,
To enter the field of ministry?"
Not knowing what the future may hold,
Trying desperately to do as I am told.
Asking, "Lord, am I good enough?"
I don't know if I can be that tough.
To carry the weight of others,
The burdens of my sisters and brothers.
I asked, "Lord, what if I fail?"
He said, "Child why feel so frail?
You can get all the strength you'll ever need,
From the One I gave and sent to bleed.
Rejoice! For the battle is won,
You know death could never defeat my Son!"

Simple Plan

A humble common man,
With a very simple plan.
Love your enemy as your friend,
It looked like the cross was the end.
But it was only the beginning,
To save us from all our sinning.
Up from the tomb He arose,
You over Himself He chose.
He has a gift that is truly free,
Only in Him is total victory!

Think Again

The Lord keeps blessing me time after time,
By letting me put my feelings down in rhyme.
These are not meaningless words in a verse,
They really can save you from a curse.
Listen carefully to these words as you read,
I pray that they will make you take heed.
If you don't know Jesus as your Savior,
Please take time to change your behavior.
Give to your brother when he is in need,
It is the lost sheep of the world we must feed.
Every day we must praise His holy name,
Because His love for us is always the same.
To escape the torture of hell's eternal burning,
We must always for the Lord's favor be yearning.
Without Jesus you can never ever win,
If you think you can—you better think again.

The Power of His Presence

The power of His presence,
Explains the very essence.
Of why we are here,
To worship, serve, and fear.
The One and Only true Lord,
Whose blood for us poured.
To save us from our sin,
The victory we can win.
Only if we choose to follow,
Our pride we must swallow.
To feel the power of the King,
He must be the Lord of everything.

Commitment

Commitment is what the Lord is looking for,
He is standing in front of an open door.
He doesn't want to be part of a casual affair,
You need to trust Him with every care.
It's not enough just to show up on Sunday,
We need to seek Him in every possible way.
If you are one who has put God in a box,
Watch out! satan can be as sly as a fox.
He has lulled you into a false sense of security,
He made you lose sight of Jesus and His purity.
If you think by sitting in a pew you have satan beat,
Friend all you're really doing is taking up a seat.
So if you've stifled God please free your church,
So they will no longer have to search.
For the glory of God's holy face,
Please return Him to His rightful place.

Prayer Is the Key

You must know He is always listening,
His throne and crown in Heaven glistening.
Prayer is the one and only key,
That can set your troubled heart free.
He knows what is on your mind,
His heart always so open and kind.
But nothing for you can be done,
Until you go to Him thru the Son.
Bow your head and close your eyes,
Because to Him you can tell no lies.
He knows every thought you think,
Always there when you start to sink.
So take to Him your worries and cares,
For He will answer all of your prayers.

With Him

With Him you can walk down any road,
Trusting Jesus with your heavy load.
Knowing that with Him,
You will never be "out on a limb."
Faith alone is not enough,
So make sure you have the right stuff.
You must in Him truly believe,
To avoid the one who tries to deceive.
He will never let you down,
Even when you feel you're about to drown.
Call on Him—He's always there,
To answer even your smallest prayer.
So come to Jesus and be all you can be,
Because with Him you will succeed eternally.

Don't Forget to Ask

Standing at my life's crossroad,
Struggling with my heavy load.
Not knowing which way to turn,
Don't know if I'll ever learn.
I can't do it all on my own,
Forgetting that I'm never alone.
All I have to do is simply ask,
And He will help with every task.
My Best Friend is always there,
I know He does truly care.
He wants to help with everything,
So to Him I will always cling.
Jesus will deliver me from every snare,
If I just take it to Him in prayer.

Jesus Is the Answer

Jesus is the answer today and every day,
He will never expect you to try to repay.
Any of the blessings He gives to you,
There is nothing you can't do.
If you truly believe in Him,
He is there when things get grim.
To comfort and lift you up,
And refill your empty cup.
Years ago on the cross His blood poured,
So that today and always He could be our Lord.
Three days later He rose from the dead,
Satan and his demons that day must dread.
To see Him in all his glory and power,
From His eternal light they must forever cower.
Jesus is the answer and all that we need,
So open your heart and let Him sow His seed.

These last few are dedicated to the one who invited me to church. God used her faithfulness to start my *ripple zone*.

My Gift

I am so proud to call you my wife,
Surely God is who brought you into my life.
As I see the strength of your devotion grow,
There is no doubt I will always know.
That your love for me is forever true,
Reflected daily in the little things you do.
You truly are a special gift from above,
An expression to me of the Father's love.
So don't ever think I don't care,
My love for you is always there.
To lift and comfort in all of life's strife,
My partner, my friend, my beautiful wife.

Can't Find the Words

How can I find the words to say,
The way you make me feel every day?
The sparkle you have put in my eyes,
You know I can never tell you lies.
The love you have stirred deep in my heart,
Like when you call me your "Sweet-tart."
The joy we share when you touch my hand,
Thank God our life together He has planned.
The empty places you somehow replaced,
My hopes and dreams are now embraced.
Making everyday experiences seem brand new,
My life just wouldn't be the same without you.

A Promise

On the first day I met you,
I never could have knew.
All the happiness waiting for us,
If we could get past everyone's fuss.
Why can't they just understand,
What happens when I hold your hand?
All the joy and pride I feel,
They have to know my love is real.
Never getting a second glance,
All I asked for is just a chance.
So when they tell you we should be done,
Remember—you only have to answer to One.
Cause Baby I can promise you this,
My love for you—you'll never miss.

My Love, My Life

From the moment I first saw you I knew,
My search was finally over—it had to be you.
Your laugh, your smile, your sweet gentle touch,
I never thought I could love someone so much.
In the middle of my day thoughts of you on my mind,
A love like yours I never dreamed I would find.
Thinking of you always brings a smile to my face,
The happiness we've shared I could never replace.
I pray you will always be by my side,
That as one in God's grace we will abide.
You'll never ever know what you truly mean to me
My friend, my love, my life, my sanity.

Forever Trapped

Feeling your breath on my face,
I can think of no other place.
That I would ever want to be,
Forever trapped in the web of your beauty.
As your hand gently touches mine,
My heart races searching for a sign.
Is the answer yes or is it no?
Is your love for me truly so?
Then I see it in your eyes,
For that is where the answer lies.
They tell me your love is as true,
As the love that I feel for you.

Always and Forever

Always so gentle and so kind,
Forever you are on my mind.
Always helping me to succeed,
Forever giving just what I need.
Always making my happiness mount,
Forever on my love you can count.
Always will I be here for you,
Forever supporting the things you do.
Always thankful you are mine,
Forever in my eyes you are so fine.
Always I need you by my side,
Forever to be my beautiful bride.

Because of You

Because of you I walk down a different road,
Much more capable of handling life's heavy load.
I never thought I could feel this way,
Somehow you've reshaped this lump of clay.
There's no way I can explain the joy you bring,
Hoping to my side you will always cling.
Don't know why these feelings keep pouring out,
Something to do with you I have no doubt.
You move me in ways I never dreamed of,
I'll be with you forever and always my love.
With just a wink or that special look,
I know you can read me like a book.
Always knowing what's on my mind,
Full of love, passion, and always so kind.
Making time for me even when I am a pest,
Never letting me feel like I'm second best.
I never dreamed a smile and a touch,
Could move a man like me so much.
I know it was you that I must meet,
Because of you my life is complete.

Searching for Answers

The Lord sent you to me for a reason,
I hope it is to be with me every season.
Now that you have returned Him to number One,
And my new Christian life has just begun.
We must do what we both know is right,
Even though it won't be an easy fight.
I know the Spirit in you is strong,
When you listen He will help you do no wrong.
Not knowing what the future may hold,
We can only put our faith in the Lord.
He will guide and show us the way,
To follow and heed His will every day.
So for now we must trust and pray,
That He will give us the answers someday.

Someday

Someday maybe you will understand,
All the emotions you hold in your hand.
Whenever I see your face I always smile,
If only it could last for more than just a while.
You have made such an impact on my life,
A friend I needed in my time of strife.
How can I even try to repay?
What you mean to me I dare not say.
My buddy, my pal, my very best friend,
I'll always be with you even till the end.
The sound of your voice makes my heart sing,
It helps to heal and calm everything.
Your inner beauty is matched only by your outer,
My ways I must change—no more a doubter.
My search has been so toiled and long,
Finally—one who strives to do no wrong.
I know for now I must bide my time,
To have what I know will someday be mine.
So now I hope and wait for the day,
When somehow you will feel the same way.
Someday…

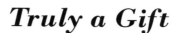

Truly a Gift

With each passing day it seems,
The Lord fulfills more of my dreams.
He brought you into my life,
I hope someday to be my wife.
He said, "This is my beautiful gift to you,"
Chris, you know I will always be true.
Just having you by my side,
Makes my heart swell with endless pride.
You can't imagine the joyous way I feel,
All my hopes and dreams have become real.
Ever since the day you said yes,
And I no longer had to guess.
Our souls have been connected at the heart,
I pray our paths will never ever part.
When I look into your beautiful eyes of brown,
I know nothing in this world can keep me down.

About the Author

James (Jim) Hartsock resides in rural Tuscarawas County, Ohio, with his wife, Chris, and son, Caleb. He has two daughters (Amanda and Sarah) and two granddaughters (Serenity and Karsen). He has been a lifelong resident of Central Ohio except for the four years he served in the United States Marine Corps. Jim enjoys being involved in the children's ministry at his church. This has led to different roles such as Sunday school teacher, junior high youth group leader, and Bible school volunteer. Currently he loves being *papaw* to his beautiful granddaughters.

CPSIA information can be obtained
at www.ICGtesting.com
Printed in the USA
FFHW020239050419
51468894-56922FF

9 781644 923283